Dealing with Emotions

SCATTERING THE CLOUDS

Ringu Tulku Rinpoche

Edited by Mary Heneghan and Marion Knight

Bodhicharya
PUBLICATIONS
Awaken the heart by opening the mind

First Published in 2012 by
BODHICHARYA PUBLICATIONS
24 Chester Street, Oxford, OX4 1SN, United Kingdom.
www.bodhicharya.org   email: publications@bodhicharya.org

ISBN 978-0-9534489-9-9
Second Edition. 2013

Edited by Mary Heneghan, Marion Knight and Ringu Tulku.

'*How to transform emotions into wisdom*' teachings given at Samye Dzong, Barcelona, Spain,
November 1997: transcribed and first edited by Gabriele Hollmann. Second edit by
Marion Knight and Mary Heneghan.

'*How to deal correctly with emotions*' teachings given at Dharma-Tor, Germany, April 2003:
transcribed by Keith Carr. Second edit by Mary Heneghan.

Bodhicharya Publications team, for this book: Tim Barrow; Annie Dibble; Marita Faaberg;
Margaret Ford; Mary Heneghan; Marion Knight; Pat Little; Eric Masterton; Rachel Moffitt;
Jet Mort; Pat Murphy; Paul O'Connor; Minna Stenroos; Claire Trueman; David Tuffield.

Typesetting & Design by Paul O'Connor at Judo Design, Ireland.
Cover Image: '*Clouds over the Atlantic*' - ©2012 Paul O'Connor
Printed on recycled paper by Imprint Digital, Devon, UK.

THE HEART WISDOM SERIES
BY RINGU TULKU RINPOCHE

The Ngöndro
Foundation Practices of Mahamudra

From Milk to Yoghurt
A Recipe for Living and Dying

Like Dreams and Clouds
Emptiness and Interdependence, Mahamudra and Dzogchen

Dealing with Emotions
Scattering the Clouds

Journey from Head to Heart
Along a Buddhist Path

Riding Stormy Waves
Victory over the Maras

Contents

'*Wheresoever is human emotion, there is sentient life;*
wheresoever is sentient life, there are the five elements, there is space;
and in so far as my compassion is co-extensive with space,
it pervades all human emotion.'

Yeshe Tsogyal [1]

Editors' Preface

Yeshe Tsogyal gave us these words in one of her songs of realisation. She was a disciple of Guru Padmasambhava, and her name is synonymous with the great ocean of primordial, natural wisdom. It is this ocean of wisdom that her words of support come from.

Everyone longs for happiness but we all experience problems and difficulties. The teachings presented as this Heart Wisdom book offer us a pathway to address this. They show us how we can work directly with our emotions and bring skill and insight to our experience of life. They encourage us that it is possible to shape our actions more freely to create more widespread and lasting happiness.

Ringu Tulku explains how we gain insight into the origin of our emotions and their impact on ourselves and others, through observing and acknowledging our habitual tendencies as they arise. A crucial step on the journey is to come into honest contact with whatever emotions are arising in us; we need to see them, feel them and accept they are happening.

Many layers of reaction tend to arise instantaneously, obscuring the simple emotions we initially experience. These include judgement, denial, sensation-seeking and believing we are different or better than others and do not have usual and common emotions. They become habitual strategies by which we avoid our emotions. What we need to do is recognise and accept what is there as a starting point. Then we can decide what we are going to do about it.

Ringu Tulku describes how we can start to address our emotions through cultivating a positive attitude and practising meditation and mindfulness. As our mind becomes calmer through these practices, there is more ease in our lives and we have more space to diffuse agitated emotions and the entanglements they create.

Lasting transformation, however, will only come once we start to deeply understand our true nature and the nature of how things really are. The practice of insight meditation leads us to see that all experience originates in the mind. We come to see that our minds and experience can be freed, because of the fluidity and clarity that are inherent qualities of mind. As we let go of negative emotions within awareness, they dissolve and give rise instead to the experiential knowing or insight that is wisdom. This is transforming emotions into wisdom.

We may still have a tendency to hold on to our emotions, as if we think they are providing the colour or 'juice' of our life. What these teachings suggest is that the real juice of life - lasting happiness and joy for ourselves and others - comes from developing pure, unconditional love and compassion, and connecting to the wisdom that lies behind the play of the emotions. This is 'the middle way', not a monochrome existence but a freer way of being: we are freed to join our experience directly with our senses, the vibrancy of our environment and the people we share our lives with.

In this book, Ringu Tulku looks at our negative emotions, how more positive counterparts may be brought out and how we can release emotions to reveal our innate wisdom. He provides guidance for this gradual process and uses stories to illustrate points along the way.

We can only put these teachings into practice step by step. Ultimately, though, there is no emotion that cannot be released into its wisdom counterpart and there is no limit to the love and compassion we can develop. And these practices have the potential to completely transform our lives.

Mary Heneghan & Marion Knight
Oxford, June 2012

All Buddhist teachings and practices are actually only concerned with and aimed at dealing with negative emotions. Guru Padmasambhava said that when the kleshas are finished, then there is no more Dharma to practice. That is to say, if you have done away with your negative emotions, then your Dharma practice is completed.

Our Situation

To what end are we striving?

The main purpose of how we live, and of spiritual practice in particular, is that we are trying to do something that will bring us more happiness, greater well-being and a better situation than we have at present. Ultimately, the aim of spiritual practice is to bring us to a state where we will have complete freedom from problems and complete joy and satisfaction. It is for this purpose and towards that end that we are striving, both in the long term and in the short term. This is regarded as a basic principle and is the basic approach of Buddhism.

This is a universal way as well as the Buddhist way. Wanting something happy, joyful and satisfactory - these are the aspirations of all people. We ask ourselves: 'How can I accomplish this? What can I do so that I can be happy and have good things happen to me?' This is the main objective of all living beings. We are always doing something, always trying something, always running after something in the pursuit of happiness and well-being in order to rid ourselves of problems.

We think, '*This* is what brings me pleasure or happiness.' And we try and try until we get what we are running after - only to find, after we have succeeded, that we are still not very happy. We try again and finally get something else, only to discover that we are still not content. This is the way we are, always running after or running away from something. We run after money; we run after jobs; we run after all different kinds of things. The real question is whether or not any of these things really brings us more permanent, lasting peace; more happiness and satisfaction. This is the very serious question that we must ask - 'What *will* bring me what I really want and will bring me that for the long run, not just for a short while?'

Of course, we do have to work in order to eat, in order to survive and have nice things. This is all right but is not what we are talking about here. Ultimately, we should ask ourselves: 'Toward what end am I striving? What results do I really expect? What is my real purpose in life? What is my real goal? Will I really ever achieve this goal? Is there any possibility that I can be completely free from all troubles and problems, and feel completely satisfied and happy? Or is there no possibility? I am always doing the same things: eating, sleeping, getting up, working. One day I will die, and then it is finished. Is this all there is to life, or is there more to it? Is there a way of finding a deeper state of being?'

These are the main questions we should ask and this is where the different spiritual teachings come in. The Buddha said there *is* something we can achieve, something *can* happen and something *can* be changed. Something can be changed completely, so that we can reach a state of mind where there are no frustrations, tensions, sufferings and pain; a state of mind in which there is complete peace, complete satisfaction and complete joy. It is possible. This is the main proposal of the Buddha. It can happen to me and it can happen to everybody.

I don't think there is anybody who really wishes bad for themselves. However, there are some people who don't like themselves. Sometimes people even say, 'I hate myself.' But in a way, I don't think hating yourself really comes from wishing bad for yourself. Rather, it comes from wishing too much good for yourself.

You wish that you were very, very good, very well off, very highly qualified. You have such high expectations of yourself, you expect everything to be perfect. Then, when you see that in reality you are not that perfect, you don't like yourself and even scorn yourself: 'I should be like that, why am I not like that?' Then you become frustrated.

This is the same frustration you feel when you expect good things from somebody else which they could not live up to. Our way of seeing is totally comparative or relative. We don't realise what our level of expectation is when we compare ourselves with others and make many assumptions about how things 'should be'.

Once, a couple came to me with their child. The child was maybe ten or twelve years old. The parents were very worried. They told me, 'Our child thinks that he will have a short life, that he will not live long. Can you say some prayers? Can you talk to him? We are quite lost over it.' They came and we talked and I asked the child, 'How long do you think you will live?' The child answered, 'Maybe around seventy years.' The parents were very relieved! The child had the idea that to live for seventy years is a very short life.

It is an important matter for us, the way we compare everything. People feel they are not good enough or hate themselves only because they are comparing themselves with others. It is our standard way to see things, to compare them. And if our references are too high, we become frustrated. But if we try to accept the way we are, with all our problems, with all our weaknesses, then nobody needs to hate him or herself.

The basis of negative emotions is fear

The basis of all negative emotions is fear, fear of getting something that we don't want, or of not getting something that we want. Because of all our problems and suffering and dissatisfaction we are always looking forward to something and so therefore we experience fear. Attachment also comes from fear because attachment is the state of holding on to something. We think, 'This is the thing I want. If I don't have this, if I don't hold on to this, then something terrible is going to happen!' Therefore, even attachment comes from fear.

Why do we feel anger? When something we want, or something nice, is being taken away, or when we don't get something we were looking forward to, then we feel angry. If something I don't like is happening or something I like is not happening, then I feel angry.

In the same way, why do we feel jealousy? Jealousy, or envy, also comes from fear. Pride, too, comes from fear, where there is the demand that I must be better than others or I will be nothing. All this comes from the feeling of insecurity which is based on fear.

Why is there so much war in the world and so much aggression? Everybody is basically selfish to some extent. We think, 'I like this. I would do anything to keep or to get this for myself.' But why do we harbour such selfishness? Selfishness comes from the fear that if I don't do this thing then something very negative will occur. I feel I must push myself to be strong and do this and do that and I force things. Even if I am sick or unwell I push myself. Even though I may not like it, I must push and get ahead. All these kinds of thoughts are based upon fear. There can't be anyone who is completely unselfish, because it is impossible unless one has become free from fear.

So, from the Buddhist point of view, we ask, 'Is it really possible to get rid of all the fear?' All negative emotions are very much based upon feelings of insecurity and fear. And fear is based on aversion and attachment:

- Aversion springs from the thought that 'This is coming and it is very bad. It is not nice and I don't like it.'
- Attachment springs from the thought that 'This is coming and I like it. This is very good and I must hold onto it.'

Therefore, as long as our state of mind is in the grip of fear, we are bound to suffer: We are bound to have problems. We are bound to be sad. We are bound to have anger. We are bound to have frustrations. We are bound to have all the tensions and negative things we actually do not like.

The main teaching of the Buddha, the main practice of the Dharma, is that there is a possibility to rid ourselves of fear. There is a possibility that we can transform our state of mind. First we need to see this as a possibility. We need to see that all this fear, all this aversion and attachment and all these expectations, are based upon a wrong way of seeing. They are based upon not knowing who I am and what I am in relation to others.

Because of this, I make the assumption that this is me and those are the others, and that anything that happens is either *for* or *against* me. When we work from this assumption, which is very delicate and founded upon insecurity, we are always afraid that something will happen. We always fear losing ground.

Wisdom

Fear and the resulting emotions are all based on our confused understanding, which is basic *ignorance of ourselves*. When we see this completely and directly, experientially and not just on an intellectual level, then we see the way we are, our true nature, what I call 'me'. If we can see this completely clearly, without any doubts and through direct experience, then it is possible to change our way of seeing generally and our ways of reacting towards others.

Real wisdom in the Buddhist sense is the ability to clearly see yourself: who you are, what you are, completely, without any veils and without any confusion. The difference between wisdom and knowledge is that knowledge is knowing something about something, whereas wisdom is seeing things clearly, experientially and from within.

Once we arrive at this wisdom, this is the stage at which we can rid ourselves of fear because we know that there is really nothing that can be destroyed, nothing that can be threatened, nothing that can be completely bad. The basis of the fear is not there anymore. When we understand and see ourselves completely, then, at that time, it is possible to transform negative emotions into wisdom.

When that happens, then it is said that we have no more problems, because the basis of our problems are founded in thoughts such as 'If this comes, it is very nice. If that comes, it is very bad.' When these kind of thoughts are no longer there, we see that things just come and go, like the clouds in the sky. Whether the clouds are there or not, it doesn't make any difference to the sun. If you understand yourself completely, you see that you are like the sun. If the clouds are there, it is nice. If the clouds are not there, it is also nice.

In the Vajrayana and Mahayana traditions, wisdom means seeing oneself clearly, completely and truly. And this is regarded as the one and only tool, or instrument, or technique, or truth, through which one can really and completely transform. As long as you don't understand yourself completely, as long as you don't see your true nature completely, then you are always bothered and suffering and fear is there. If you see yourself completely and clearly, then whatever arises in the mind, whatever comes and goes, does not change anything. Your way of seeing changes. It is like looking from 'above'.

That is why, in the Vajrayana, especially in the instructions on Mahamudra and similar teachings, the introduction to the nature of mind is emphasised. And that is also why it is said that it is possible to change, it is possible to improve, it is possible for us to get out of this kind of bondage. We can become completely free - free from our fears, free from our negative emotions and free from all our sufferings - if we have complete understanding and direct experience of wisdom.

It is not easy to see this freedom, though, because we are so entangled in layer upon layer of our assumptions, our concepts, our ideas and our habits and patterns. This is all due to the way we think and the way we habitually see ourselves. We may have a little intellectual understanding but this knowledge doesn't change us because we are so accustomed to being the way we are.

The Buddhist view is that we are naturally completely free. But we have built up so many concepts, patterns and habits around ourselves based on the wrong way of seeing, that it takes a lot of endeavour, a great deal of practice and a very strong direct experience to get through these layers and see ourselves clearly. It is through Dharma teachings and different practices that the Buddha recommended; it is through explanations and experiencing contact with enlightened beings, that we may penetrate these layers and reach an understanding of our true nature.

The Buddha presented many different teachings for different kinds of people. He said that it is not possible to give only one recommendation for everybody to follow, because we are all at many different levels and have varied dispositions. The main thing is to completely understand ourselves, to see ourselves clearly and truly; to see the real, basic and true primordial nature of ourselves. That is all. But it is not easy to do.

So these many different people need many ways and means, and different stages of these ways and means. The students needed all the different kinds of teachings defined and categorised somehow, so the Buddha categorised the three yanas and the nine yanas and so on. There are actually countless paths but they were categorised for the students. The Buddha himself said, 'I have presented 84,000 different varieties of ways and paths in my life.'

Many different approaches are necessary. Each individual has to find and go through his or her own patterns and habits and then work on them. It is not something that anybody else can just give you – 'Oh, this is the teaching. Through this all the problems are finished!' It is not like that. Rather, it is work we need to do within ourselves. We have to decide to make a commitment to work on our own patterns and habits and to try to work through them.

In a nutshell, all Buddhism - maybe every spiritual path - is actually directed towards being able to see what we call 'wisdom'. That is the real goal and the true purpose of all practices. We are only able to proceed step-by-step, according to our level, our understanding, our experience.

The main thing is that we need to understand that we have to start where we are. We cannot imagine we can start from anywhere else other than where we are, for the simple reason we are not there. We have to see ourselves as we are now. This means that we have to accept our ignorance and our problems. We have to accept ourselves as we are. This is where we have to start from. It doesn't mean that we cannot improve - we can!

It is very important to know the problems and weaknesses that we, as well as others, have. If you expect everybody to be perfect, then you are heading for a big shock. We need to understand, right from the beginning: I am as I am, I am not perfect, I have lots of problems, lots of weaknesses, lots of things to work on, to practice.

We can understand that it is the same for everybody, that nobody is completely unselfish; nobody is completely good, nobody is completely perfect; we are all trying our best. When I understand this, if I meet somebody who is not that nice, then that is all right because I can appreciate that he or she is trying his or her best and I can feel better about it.

The story of Valmiki

The story of Valmiki may help us to understand these points.

Valmiki is said to be the first poet of India, and lived a long, long time ago. It so happens that he was a robber, a highway-man. He would sit in wait in the forest and rob anybody who passed by. One day he was waiting in the woods when he spotted a Rishi, a person dedicated to a spiritual path.

Valmiki stopped him and demanded, 'Give me everything, otherwise I will kill you!'

The Rishi responded, 'Well, I have nothing, but you can take whatever you like. But why are you doing this, why are you like this?

Why are you not working or doing something else?'

Valmiki replied, 'I am doing this because of my family, to support my family and to support my parents. Anyway, it is none of your business. You just give me everything.'

The Rishi said, 'It is all right. I will give you everything. I really don't have that much, but you can take everything. But tell me, why are you doing this negative and bad thing for your family, your children and parents? It is not nice.'

Valmiki replied, 'This is my profession. I do this for all of them.'

The Rishi continued, 'But then you have lots of bad karma by doing these negative things... I am sure your parents are not going to share your bad karma. Your wife is not going to share your bad karma. Your children are not going to share your bad karma. They would all be ashamed.'

At this, Valmiki became very angry, 'No, you are wrong! They are going to share my karma because I am only doing this for them.'

The Rishi replied, 'No, I am sure that they will not share your karma. You just go back and ask them whether they are willing to share your bad karma or not.'

Valmiki answered, 'Well, you will run away during that time.'

But the Rishi responded, 'No, no, just bind me to the tree.'

Valmiki tied the Rishi to the tree and went to ask his father, 'You know, I am doing lots of negative things to get food for the family. It might have a negative result in the next life. Are you going to share that?'

And his father said, 'Oh no, no, no! I am not going to share any of that. I am very old. I am dying now. You are supposed to feed us and look after the family and the way you do it is up to you. Your bad karma is your responsibility and I cannot share it with you even if I wanted to.'

Next, Valmiki went to his mother and she reacted in a similar way. Immediately, he went to his wife but she too was not ready to share his bad karma. Then he went to his children and they were even less ready to share his bad karma.

Valmiki was very shocked. Returning to the Rishi, he untied him and said, 'What you said is true. They are not willing to share my bad karma. So, what shall I do?'

To this the Rishi replied, 'Oh, you can do whatever you like, you can carry on as you are or you can practise, you can purify your bad karma.'

Valmiki said, 'All right, what is it that I should be doing? You teach me how to meditate and I am going to practise.'

So the Rishi taught him how to meditate and Valmiki sat under a tree and meditated. He was such a strong man, such a determined person, that once he began to meditate he soon went into samadhi.

Slowly, slowly, over time, the ants came and built an anthill over his body. Then, after I don't know how many months or how many years, when he came back to consciousness, he looked around and saw that his entire body was covered by the anthill. There were only two small holes through which he could look out. Through the holes he saw two birds peacefully gliding in the sky. Valmiki felt so good and so joyful that he uttered a verse that is said to be the first stanza of the great Indian epic, the Ramayana, which he later composed.

Working on ourselves

Unless you first start to change yourself and do something differently, you cannot make others do so. It starts with yourself. Peace starts with yourself. War starts with yourself. And the transformation of the world starts with yourself. So, therefore, if each and everybody tries to do something to become even a little bit better, a little bit changed, a little bit transformed, then actually to change the world is not necessarily so very difficult.

If each and everybody on this earth made a resolution that 'From tomorrow I am not going to harm anybody; I am going to be friendly towards everybody' - there would be peace the next day. It's not that difficult to bring peace if we really want to, but it has to come from our heart and from all of us. It won't come from 'somebody has to do it' but from 'I have to do it'.

It is said that there was once a priest, somewhere in Scotland. He was an old man and just before he passed away, he asked his followers to write a statement on his tombstone where he was to be buried. In essence it was something like this:

"When I was young I was very enthusiastic and I wanted to change the whole world. So I prayed, 'Please, Lord God, give me the wisdom and the power to change the whole world.' I tried my best but as I grew older I found that nothing had changed. Then I came to understand that actually I have to try to change my near and dear ones first, and if they change, the world might change taking them as an example. I prayed to the Lord God 'Please give me the power and wisdom to change my near and dear ones.' And I tried my best again.

When I became very old, however, I found that still nothing had changed. Then I came to know that actually I must change myself first. If I changed myself, maybe some of my near and dear ones would change taking that as an example. And then, taking them as an example, maybe the world would start to change. Now I pray to the Lord God 'Please give me the strength and wisdom to change myself.' But alas, now it is too late."

Once I was in Ireland, and somebody asked this question: 'How can I forgive the people who have done such damage to me and my people? It is not possible to feel compassion for the other side, for our enemies, because we have suffered so much. How can I forget that?'

I said, 'Okay, you have suffered, your people have suffered; but what about the other side?'

It is just the same if you are fighting with anybody. For instance, somebody says something or does something not so nice to me. I think 'this person is not very nice to me', so the next time I do something similar to him. Then the next time he comes and does a little bit more and I say, 'Why are you doing that?' and maybe I give him a blow. And then the next time he brings his friends and they beat me up. And then my people come and beat them up. And then a whole war has started.

Now, nobody can stop it because my people think, 'Why did they do this to us?' And their people think, 'Why did they do that?' So it goes on. Now maybe I am killed in the process and maybe some of them are killed. So nobody can forgive and it goes on and on and on. Hatred begets hatred.

We think, 'My people have suffered so much, all these things cannot be wiped out. I cannot forget that.' The other people think the same way. But most of the time I forget that the other people have gone through the same problems, the same suffering, the same fears. So it's equal. But if somebody doesn't stop it, it will go on and on and both sides will continue to suffer.

If you are wise, you don't want to suffer and you don't want your people to suffer. So, therefore, you have to stop the fighting. The only way we can stop is to say, 'Okay, we have suffered, they have suffered, but at some point we have to stop all this.'

Whoever can stop it is actually the winner. Whoever can stop the ping-pong of hatred is the winner because then both sides win. Yes we have suffered but the other side has also suffered. If I don't do something negative or hateful right from the beginning, if I can stop myself, then that is even better.

Forgiveness comes from here. It is not about thinking, 'I am very holy, I am so compassionate, I forgive everything.' It's not like that. Forgiveness happens because it's good for me and good for others. It's wise. It is the only way to stop continual negative things happening. So, therefore, it has to be done; there is no other way. This is wisdom.

Negative Emotions

Looking at negative emotions

We have been speaking about wisdom because we are looking at *how to transform emotions into wisdom*. Therefore, we have tried to look and see what wisdom is in the Buddhist sense, which is actually nothing other than completely understanding yourself. This is the key thing. The whole tradition of debating in the Tibetan style is actually designed to uncover exactly this – have you seen yourself clearly or not? If you do not see yourself clearly first, then you will lose the debate. This is the traditional way of saying it.

The Tibetan way of debating is quite specific. One person sits in front of everyone and lots of people ask them questions; they ask question after question until, in the end, 'I am forced to eat my own words' (which is a Tibetan saying). If first I answer 'yes', then the people have to ask questions until I say 'no'. When I answer with a 'no,' then I am defeated.

In Buddhist etymology we speak about 'What is this?' 'What is the thing here?' 'What is the real nature of things?' That is what we try to find out directly. This is the Buddhist way of thinking and experiencing, to see things clearly and to see everything exactly *as it is*, in its natural state. This is about recognising ourselves, or rather not just recognising, but seeing ourselves fully cleared or purified of our coverings or stains or obscurations.

By 'obscurations' we mean anything that obscures and prevents us from seeing something. If I want to see this Buddha image and there is something in between, then what is in between obscures the Buddha from my vision. Therefore, whatever is obscuring and preventing me from seeing, whatever is hiding the way it is, the way my true nature is, then this is an obscuration.

In Buddhism, we speak about two obscurations, two things that really prevent us from seeing our true nature directly. The first is known as the *kleshas*, which we often call the negative emotions, and the second is the *she bye drib pa* or the habitual tendencies. These two obscurations hinder us from seeing our true nature.

When wisdom is realised, it does not just point to the absence of obscurations, or the absence of problems and suffering. Our true nature is always there, hidden beneath the obscurations. Our true nature is fully positive. All the good and positive qualities are naturally and intrinsically always there. What does this really mean?

When someone becomes enlightened, they have cleared all their obscurations and they have, through this, gained complete wisdom. He or she has become free from all problems and has gained complete joy, complete happiness. All the positive qualities were naturally there all the time, buried beneath the obscurations.

If I am agitated and my mind is frustrated, panicky and negative, then I feel very bad. But if I can get rid of these feelings, if I pacify my mind, if I make my mind calm and peaceful, then not only do the agitations and frustrations subside, but joy and happiness come up naturally and on their own. The more peaceful the mind becomes, the more joyful I become. The more the negative aspects subside, the more positive aspects come up.

When your mind becomes a little bit calmer, then your mind becomes much clearer. Qualities like intuition and intuitive power become stronger when your mind is calm. Even telepathy can occur when the mind becomes calm and clear.

These are the strengths of the natural quality of our consciousness, mind, or whatever you want to call it. Our consciousness is intrinsically and naturally filled with all qualities of an enlightened being. Positive qualities are not something that we need to find outside ourselves through improving or creating them. They are always naturally there. This is the Mahayana way of seeing things and also, especially, the Vajrayana way. The fully enlightened state is already there, only it is hidden by obscurations; in the same way as the sun is always shining high up in the sky even when it is obscured by clouds.

When we are underneath the clouds, then we cannot see the sun and we experience a cloudy or a rainy day. But the sun itself has not changed, nor has it been touched by the clouds at all. It has its own shining power, its clarity, and its burning heat. Its rays are always there. It has never been without its rays. It has never been without its strength and heat, even while the clouds obscure it, but only when the clouds are gone is the sun fully visible and we are able to feel its heat. While the clouds are there, the sun is not shining for us or others. In the same way, wisdom is like the sun and the obscurations are like the clouds. What we need to do is clear away the clouds. That is the whole practice.

I have already discussed the two main states of mind that obscure our natural wisdom and bring forth fear - aversion and attachment. They are both based upon ignorance. From these three basic states come the five negative emotions:

- Anger and aversion, which includes hatred, malice and aggression.
- Attachment, which includes greed, craving, strong miserliness, clinging and the inability to let go.
- Ignorance, which includes being confused, unaware and a complete dullness of the mind; not wanting to look into things. For example, we may decide to accept what others say as truth rather than use our own capacity to find out how things are.

- Jealousy, or envy, which is often very dangerous because it arises out of a mixture of both hatred and attachment. We like something and hate losing it, and therefore become angry.
- Pride, very much based upon ignorance, is a feeling of insecurity which includes a strong sense of arrogance and over-rating oneself. According to Buddhism, pride is not only about seeing oneself as the best, but also includes seeing oneself as the worst or as different to everyone else. It includes being self-absorbed in this way.

These disturbed mind states may not all be commonly called emotions. Ignorance, for instance, is not usually regarded as an emotion, but it is what we call a *klesha*. Kleshas are all states that arise and overpower our mind, causing us to experience suffering and preventing us from experiencing love, joy and happiness. This is what we need to address: *anything that arises in our mind and can create an emotion strong enough to overpower us and cause us unhappiness and suffering if we allow ourselves to be led by it.* This is what the kleshas are and this is how they obscure our natural wisdom.

Not all emotions are the same in terms of their effect; some are not as bad as others. And some are easier to deal with, while others are harder to eliminate. For instance, the Buddha taught that out of the three main kleshas, ignorance is the most basic. So if we can eradicate ignorance, then everything negative is eliminated and we will become fully enlightened.

Although the negative effect of ignorance does not seem to be that strong and is not that evident, it is all-pervasive and its influence is very serious because all disturbed emotions arise from it. But it does not cause harm directly and in this very moment. You can still have a good night's sleep even if you have not cleared all your ignorance – you can have a nice dinner, a nice day tomorrow. You can still enjoy your life. It is not the most urgent thing to eradicate.

However, ignorance is the most difficult to completely clear because it is the inner core of our obscurations and the foundation of our misunderstandings. Ignorance is the basic problem we face and as such, is something that we deal with all the time. But it won't vanish until the very last. Therefore, we need to relax a little bit about it. We must work on it constantly, but slowly and gradually.

Anger, fuelled with malice and aggression, is something we have to deal with first, because nothing good whatsoever results from this very destructive and harmful emotion. Nothing good arises for us or others from anger. If you are angry, in that moment you are not happy and the result is that you harm someone or destroy something. Even more serious are feelings of hatred and malice and wanting revenge.

The Buddha said that anger resembles fire - it is strong, flares up quickly and goes out again. Anger is therefore easier to recognise and the way it passes quickly makes it easier to deal with. If you can wait a little bit, it will pass. Anger is the first emotion that should be dealt with, because it burns you and everybody else. ·

Attachment is also very deep and very strong in human beings. It is very difficult to get rid of because it is our utmost emotion. But it has some good sides as well as bad. In a way, compassion comes a little bit from attachment. The wish to have good things for myself and others also, more or less, comes from attachment. It is when attachment turns into overtly strong clinging that it becomes negative.

These are the three basic emotions or kleshas, and each also operates at various levels. According to the Buddha, we have to deal with them in order. We have to transform hatred first: feelings of anger, malice, not forgiving, clinging to a resentful and revengeful frame of mind and all such negative dispositions. These disturbed emotions are very destructive and instantly bring on much suffering for ourselves and for others.

The general understanding from the Buddhist point of view is that we deal with emotions one by one, one after another. We start with the easy and move on to the more difficult. We move from the more understandable to the less understandable; and from the general to the more specific. Whatever is most problematic we work on first, because that is what is hurting most.

Many people perceive the sole Buddhist objective is to become enlightened and it is true that complete enlightenment is the ultimate objective - not only complete enlightenment for oneself, but for all sentient beings. But, until we reach that point, what are we supposed to do?

Too often the temporary aspect is forgotten or lost when we are discussing enlightenment, and enlightenment itself is seen as being very far off. While we may be working towards attaining this state ultimately, we should not overlook temporary objectives to simply do whatever is good and positive. We have to do good and positive things now, also, before we become enlightened.

Anger and compassion

When we say that we should work on our emotions and work on anger, what we mean is that we should not let anger totally take us over. It does not mean to say that whatever anybody does to us, whatever injustices are done, we should just take them lying down and not do anything. That is not what we are saying. What we are saying is that if somebody does something not so nice to us, we can still explain or find a just, or right, way of dealing with that.

The main thing is that we should not become a victim of our anger and suffer ourselves. This can also lead to us doing a lot of damage to others. I think it is usually something like this: people get angry when they cannot talk properly; when they cannot communicate. This leads to them feeling even more angry. Maybe they feel like, 'I cannot communicate so I just bang my table!' This doesn't help. Letting ourselves just be angry doesn't help.

Sometimes people say they cannot fight for justice if they don't get angry. But this is where the understanding is incorrect. From the Buddhist point of view, the source of both anger and compassion can be the same. The same situation that causes anger can also give rise to compassion. It is said that whether compassion arises, or anger arises, depends on how we see things, where we focus. When we see something happening that should not happen, whether it is to us or to somebody else, then either we can become angry or we can have compassion.

If we focus on the person: '*This person* has done that', then we become angry. The focus is directed towards the person or people, and concentrates on seeing them in a bad light. Then you might want to crush them or harm them or wish them bad things, and that becomes anger. But if your focus goes to the cause, the situation that is happening, and you see it should be changed and should not happen, then compassion is what is arising in that moment. Your focus is not this person or those people, but the situation that has to be changed. You do not have a harmful or malevolent wish but a more beneficial, benevolent desire that this should not happen.

When you see something going wrongly and anger arises, this anger can become stronger and stronger until it is very powerful. When you become angry like this you can become very strong. Even if five people try to hold you, you cannot be held back! You walk about quickly and a certain kind of strength builds up more and more strongly. But you lose your reasoning power. The anger takes over you and you no longer think rationally. You start talking and say much more than you meant to and you exaggerate things. If you say something like that when you are angry, you almost always have a reason to regret it afterwards. Any action you take is also like that, exaggerated, because you have lost your rationality. With that power or energy of anger you always destroy yourself and others. You cannot do anything positive.

This can happen during demonstrations, for example. The demonstration starts peacefully and for a good cause but after some time anger takes over and then it becomes destructive. The force or strength that is generated by anger is not actually useful because it is beyond control and is not rational. It can easily lead to doing something not right and not good.

Then how is it afterwards? Because anger is like a flame, it flares up very quickly and then it also dies down again very quickly. After strong anger you become totally exhausted. When you are angry you may go red and blue and all these things but afterwards you become very tired very quickly. All your energy is actually exhausted. So this energy is not useful and is not something with which you can pursue an important cause.

So, we can see that anger is not a good thing, even to fight injustice. It does not work. We should try to generate compassion instead so that when we see something happening that should not be happening we can try to do something to change the situation. We are not against anybody. We just need to focus ourselves on changing the situation. When you have that attitude and focus, you don't need to be angry or hateful. You can have understanding and patience so that you persistently work to get rid of the problems and suffering. Even if it is not nice and you have to go through certain problems, you are ready to do that. That is compassion.

Sometimes people ask, 'When we don't express our emotions, are we repressing them?' Like anger, for instance. We feel angry but we don't want to express it: 'I am angry but I don't want to show it.' Then it can be repressed which is not good for us. This is very important to understand, because what repressed means is that you don't let it go, you hold on to it. You don't show any signs of it. You don't hit somebody or bang the door or throw plates or something like that. But you still keep it. That is repression.

Repressing is holding on to the disturbed feeling, without letting it go. And it is quite possible to do that after expressing the disturbed feeling as well. What we are trying to learn here is not to hold on to the emotion. If you express an emotion, it is not good, but it is not *that* bad. If something happens and you become angry and you go red and green and shout and throw a plate or bang the door, it is not the worst thing. But if you keep the anger, that is much worse, because that is making it into hatred. Hatred is holding on to the anger. When we are talking about how to deal with emotions, we are not only talking about expression, we are talking about how we hold on to an emotion or do not hold on to it. The whole practice is learning how to not hold on to emotions.

Attachment and loving-kindness

It may be obvious how aversion brings suffering, because when we don't like something that *is* aversion – we are talking about something we don't like or something we fear. Aversion is naturally regarded as an unpleasant thing. But why do we say attachment brings unhappiness, because it is about me *liking* something? I get attached to things I like. I like something and I want to have it. If I lose it, then I feel very bad.

How does that bring unhappiness? If I have it then I have the fear of losing it. If I don't have it then I want it and I have the dissatisfaction of not having it. The more attached I am, the greater my fear of losing it or of not having it. So, we can see how attachment generates fear and, therefore, aversion. That is why it can become a source of suffering.

In Buddhism we talk about disturbed, or negative, emotions and positive emotions. Some people don't like the term 'negative emotions' and prefer to use instead 'harmful emotions' or 'disturbed emotions'. What is referred to by all these terms are the emotions that create pain and suffering. The way we define negative deeds, and also positive emotions and positive deeds, is similar.

From the Buddhist point of view, actions that generate painful and unpleasant circumstances for yourself and others, because they are inspired by disturbed emotions, are the negative deeds. Positive deeds are actions that are inspired by positive emotions and that generate more peace, more kindness, better results and good feelings toward each other. Actions that generate well-being for yourself and others are called positive deeds. That is the only criteria, from the Buddhist point of view, to categorise whether an emotion or an action is positive or negative.

So what about attachment, and love or *maitrî* (*maitreya* in Sanskrit)? What is the difference between attachment and loving-kindness? It is true there is an element of attachment in compassion and loving-kindness, but the basic difference is that loving-kindness and compassion are more concerned with thinking about others. It is not so much about thinking things like, 'I need this. If I don't have it I will not be happy' or 'I need you.' When 'I' is the most important thing, then that is attachment, because it is conditional.

You might say, for example, 'I love you.' But what you mean is, 'I love you as long as you love me.' Love can turn into hatred just like that. Because the moment you don't respond to me the way that I want you to, I don't love you anymore. And it is not even just that I don't love you anymore, I *hate* you! That is how love turns into hatred so easily, because it is conditional. It is more about me. 'I' am the first thing. 'I' want it.

In real love, what we call 'pure' love or loving-kindness, you are not talking too much about yourself. The main focus is wishing good to the person you love. If something good happens to this person or they are well, this makes you feel so happy. That kind of love is not conditional. Whether this person loves you or not is not the main criteria. Just wanting good things for this person and wishing them well is the main thing. And that is loving-kindness.

The main difference is whether it is conditional and 'I' am the most important thing or whether it is not conditional and the other person is the most important thing. Of course, there is still a little bit of attachment at our level because we are samsaric beings; our mind is still a little bit confused and not able to see things completely clearly.

We run after something we desire. But 'I want' means I don't have it. If I have it, then I *have* it and I don't need to *want* it. So I can't have what I am running after. I can never have what I want, because when I have it I no longer want it, because I have it! As long as I don't have it, I want it. So, therefore, it is a problem. It is a tension. It is a cause of suffering.

That is what is happening for all of us. We look for complete satisfaction, complete happiness and complete fearlessness, but we don't get it because we are in that state of mind, we are reacting in that way. So we can see that the more we want, the more problems we have - just like the more we don't want, the more problems we have.

Attachment is a cause of suffering but it also has positive aspects because it brings love and compassion. Even the wish, 'May I and all beings become enlightened,' has an element of attachment because it is about 'I' would like to help liberate all the sentient beings. So even the Bodhisattva's attitude of compassion has an element of attachment and there is nothing wrong with that.

We have to work with attachment but we find we cannot get rid of it just like that because it is very strong. We have lots of attachment to things, attachment to people and attachment to ourselves. It can be nice to be attached, and that is okay, but it also causes problems. We don't usually lose sleep because of attachment but we might if we lost someone we had a lot of attachment to, for example.

Overall, attachment has both good sides and bad sides. It causes problems but it also brings solutions to problems.

Question: Fear

Student: If negative emotions are all based on fear, does that mean that negative emotions are a form of fear, that all the negative emotions are fear in disguise? We frequently experience fear. Is this fear we experience a form of basic duality? How do we deal with it?

Rinpoche: What I am saying is that when I feel angry, it is not fear, it is anger. But the point I am making is, *why* am I feeling angry? Either because something happened or something is about to happen that I don't like. What is it that I don't like, why don't I like something? Because I am afraid that something bad or terrible is going to happen, this is the reason I feel fear. I believe that is how fear arises. Anger is not fear, but arises from a sequence produced by fear.

If you can somehow get rid of all your fear, then there is no reason for you to be angry. This is the ultimate point: *if we can really get rid of all our fear and become free of any fear, whatever happens, nothing can bother us and we won't be unhappy or upset.* At that time, everything is all right, because we know that nothing can harm us, nothing is disagreeable, and everything can be good.

That is the Buddhist way of seeing it, that fear is generated by a wrong way of seeing things.

We are talking about the kind of fear that is the source of aversion and attachment, and if we are a good meditator, we can deal with it through meditation. The final solution is to completely make our mind calm and clear but this can take a long time. If we can completely be in the true nature of our mind then that is a deep solution and it is a long term solution. But is there a way to deal with these things at a more temporary, immediate level? How would you deal with it if you had a fear of, say public speaking or a fear of heights? How would you work with that?

The only way to do it is to face it. If you want to become a public speaker but you are afraid of speaking in front of others, you have to face it and come out in front of the audience and speak! Maybe you cannot manage even to say anything the first time but the more times you do it the easier it becomes. After all, in the end, it is essentially the same whether you are speaking to one person or ten people. It is the same with a fear of heights – you just have to climb up. The way to work with fear is to face it. There may be different ways of doing that, but the most important thing is to be able to say that whatever happens, you can accept it, you can cope with it.

I don't mean you accept in the sense that you don't do anything about something you are afraid of. If you have a fear of sickness, for example, and you get sick, you still do whatever you can to treat the sickness. We do the best we can, but it is very important to be prepared, to be able to face the worst that can happen.

I was very sick once with Tuberculosis. It is the second largest cause of death in India and Tibetans don't have any resistance to it. So I had to be a little bit prepared. I could really have died. But everybody has to die one day and acceptance of this is very important. Once you really accept it, it is okay, your fear becomes much, much less. Your pain may not be less but your fear is less. So therefore you actually experience less pain.

There is a saying in Tibetan that, 'A coward dies a hundred times a day and a brave man dies only once in his lifetime.' Everybody has to die one day so if you are not too afraid you will just die one day like everybody must, without panicking and worrying too much beforehand. But if you are already very afraid of dying, it is as if you are dying every day. There is no use in that. The main thing is to face it and accept it and be prepared.

Question: The harmfulness of kleshas

Student: The idea that the kleshas are much more harmful to us than even being tortured and killed challenges my deeply held assumption that the worst possible thing that can happen to a human being is to be killed. If we understand that the kleshas can cause interminable and unrelenting pain, whereas being killed just happens once and then it is over, can this help us become less fearful of death and realise the urgency of overcoming the negative emotions?

Rinpoche: The Buddhist way of understanding is that we have life after life after life. We die but we are born again. And how we are born again, whether we are born in a more positive state or a more negative state, depends on how we are and what state of mind we are in. So that means that the more negativity, the more kleshas, then the more likely we are to be born in a negative situation so that we suffer more.

We all have to die anyway, once in each lifetime. Whether we like it or not, we cannot 'not die'. We can die a little bit earlier, we can die a little bit later, but we all have to die. That is the process, there is no choice. We all have to die, whether we see death as a very bad thing or not such a bad thing. If there is life after dying and we are reborn, then what kind of life comes afterwards is extremely important.

The idea here though is that our present life is affected as well as any further life. If we completely give in to our disturbed emotions then we will create a lot of problems and pain for ourselves and for others in this actual lifetime. We make our life very un-enjoyable and painful and difficult. Then we will die anyway, whether we live like this or another way.

If we have strong negativity and kleshas then we will also have more fear; so we have more fear of death than if we can work to reduce our kleshas. If we can overcome the kleshas then we will have less fear or no fear and then even death becomes easy. This is what happens in this very life. After we die, if we have less klesha, then we will have a much more pleasant form of life - because the way we are and how our mind is reacting is the pattern our lives follow, both now and in future lives. If we have less klesha, then the next life can be a more positive life, whereas more klesha leads to a more negative life. This pattern goes on and on and on.

Therefore, the kleshas are much more important than death as they have a much stronger negative or positive effect. Death is something we cannot avoid – one life, one death, that is a certainty. But if we have too much emotion and negativity and kleshas then we will also have a lot of fear and aversion. This makes it more difficult in our present life and more difficult when we die and also more difficult afterwards.

So we need to work on our disturbed emotions. It is not necessary to go to all the Buddhas to ask what we need to work on - we can clearly see for ourselves what the main things are that we need to deal with and eliminate. Of course, it is not easy. It is never said that it will be easy to deal with fear or any emotion, because they have been with us for such a long time. This doesn't mean to say that they are a part of us. They are not our true nature, but we have been with them for so long that our habits have almost become our own nature. Therefore, they are very automatic. We don't need to think about or cultivate anger, for instance, because it just springs up very quickly and quite strongly. So, it is not easy to eliminate. It is easier to control than to eliminate anger.

It is good to learn to control disturbed emotions. The more we can work on them, the better it is. If we let our negative emotions control us completely, then we are lost and have no chance. Then, really, we have completely lost our freedom. We have no freedom because we are like slaves to our negative emotions. If we do whatever they command, then we will do whatever brings us suffering and problems. Therefore, we should try a little to take our lives into our own hands and free ourselves a little. The more we do so, the better it is. That's the whole understanding. How do we do this? We do a little at a time.

Where do we start?

Understand - decide - work skilfully

In order to transform our emotions and free ourselves, we need to:

- *Understand.*

  We need to understand exactly how the negative emotions operate, and we need to know that if we allow them to control and lead us, then they will cause us problems and suffering. Seeing this is the first step towards dealing with them. Being aware, knowing and recognising that I will have no freedom and will only encounter trouble if they overpower me. This is the first point we need to understand.

- *Decide.*

  We need to be convinced and confident that we will not allow ourselves to be completely overpowered by a negative emotion, otherwise we will be led by the rope. In Tibet we have yaks - wild and fierce animals. But if you put a ring through their nose and tie a rope to the ring, you can lead them wherever you want. In the same way, our emotions can lead us from our own nose. We lose control of our actions because our emotions drive them instead. Even if we know something is wrong we may be unable to choose freely not to do it.

As long as we think that the emotions are sacred and should not be touched and we always follow them, they may lead us anywhere - and then they go and desert us! We need to decide that we will not allow our negative emotions to overtake us. They have been overpowering us until now and so far things haven't gone that well. Therefore, we will not let this happen anymore. We can decide: 'I will be skilful and free myself from negative emotions.'

- *Work skilfully.*
  After such thoughts have been generated, we try to work on them. We try to work on them at different levels. It is not possible just by snapping our fingers, because we are dealing with emotions and the mind. It is not like building a house. When we build a house we stack one brick upon the other and achieve more in ten hours than in five or six hours. The mind is more subtle than that and we have to work more skilfully. If we push too hard, things go in another direction.

Emotion itself is a very strange thing. Sometimes it is said to be a little bit like a nettle. A nettle stings if you touch it. The more carefully you touch it, the more lightly you touch it, the more it stings. You can't just touch it gently. But if you hold it firmly and strongly it doesn't sting. Emotion is a little bit like that: if you know how to work with it, you are less likely to be stung. The more you hold emotions sacred, the more they boss you around and the more atrocities they can do to you. Sometimes we think too much as if, 'I feel like this so I must act upon it.' If we think like this, we will never cease to be disturbed.

Instead, we need to think that we *can* and *will* work with an emotion. But where do we start? The way of working on emotions is through our attitude, or our way of seeing things, and through meditation. We need to use meditation because we cannot totally force this work. If we think,

'Oh, I don't want this!' then whatever it is, it comes more strongly. So, we need a way of dealing with emotions that is much more subtle: not pushing away too much, not surrendering too much. And that is what meditation is based on.

Meditation: a practical learning

Meditation provides a training to get a handle on our emotions in the first place and then to work on them at more and more subtle levels. It is something we can only learn through doing, through practice. It is not something we can learn through concepts or through the intellect. We cannot just memorise it in order to understand it. We have to learn how to do it, *practically*, like learning how to play music or ride a bicycle or drive a car. The subtlety of how to do it is not even something that can be taught. It can only be learned through actually doing. You can say a lot about it. You can talk and talk and talk, but that is only talking *about* it; it is not meditation itself.

Starting is very simple actually. You need to learn how to relax first, how to relax your mind. That is not easy. The words are very easy to say 'Oh, relax!' and then I am trying to relax. But it is something that you cannot try to do, because the more you *try* the less relaxing it becomes!

It is something you have to learn from your guts; or from the bottom of your heart. From experience, you learn how to be. To relax is how to let things be. If you cannot let things be, you cannot relax. When you can let things be, then you can let your emotions and thoughts come and you can let them go. You learn how to accept that it doesn't matter whatever comes, let it come. And it doesn't matter if it goes, let it go. When you can do that, then that is meditation. Therefore, in a way, it is very easy. But everything is like that: when you know how to do something, it's easy. If you don't know how to do it, though, it is very difficult.

Meditation is begun by trying to relax your body, because the body and mind are so interconnected. They are absolutely interconnected. Whatever happens in the mind happens in the body and whatever happens in the body also completely happens in the mind. By changing our attitude and our way of thinking and way of being - our mind - we can change our body. We can affect our body a lot in this way.

For instance, it is very easy to see how someone is feeling, even when observing them from behind. In this way, if you look at how somebody in front of you is walking, you can see how they are feeling. If they are happy they will walk in an upright way and they will be looking here and there. When someone looks fixedly at one point you can tell they are chewing over a problem. If we have a problem, then all our attention goes there.

We need to learn how to relax a bit and learn how to let our mind and ourselves be more spacious. 'Spacious' means that there is room for lots of things inside. Some good things, some bad things, some nice things, and some not so nice things. When we are spacious then things can come and go.

The body and mind affect each other so much that if we can relax our body a little bit it greatly helps us to relax our mind. There are many different kinds of exercises for that purpose, including yoga and tai chi and many others. But we cannot relax our body without relaxing our mind a little bit, it is so inter-related. Sometimes people think of it as just a physical thing, to relax the body. Of course, it is a physical thing, but it is very much affected by our mind. When we try to relax our body, this means relaxing our mind actually, because clearly, when you relax your body, it has to be relaxed *with* your mind.

Much of the time our body is tensed by worry. When we relax our body, we begin to feel more relaxed. We feel 'ease,' because tension in the body comes from tension in the mind. We need to learn to meditate without trying too hard because when we try, we try by means of a kind of tension. If we tense ourselves we are not relaxed. Because we are used to doing everything by trying, we try to meditate and we cannot do it like that. You cannot try. You just have to relax. You can only allow it to happen by itself. It is not about 'doing'. It is actually 'not doing'. And that is meditation.

We are not used to relaxing, so as soon as we do we are gone, we are asleep. Sleep is a good thing, good for your body and good for your mind too. But it is not meditation. We have to relax and not fall asleep. We need to be relaxed and awake and clear. And at the same time we also allow whatever arises in our mind to arise and then to pass on. We don't try to 'manage'. We don't try to judge. When we can do that, this is more how we naturally are.

Our consciousness is naturally awake and clear and its nature is to manifest all different kinds of thoughts and emotions, all different kinds of good things and bad things, all different kinds of colours. We want to hold on to good thoughts or good emotions but we can't hold on to them because everything that appears, disappears. And we can't stop a bad experience or something that we don't want to look at, from arising. But it will also disappear.

The only problem comes when we become entangled with our experience and try to fight it or try to hold on to it. We always struggle in this way, and it is a futile struggle. Meditation is just completely letting things be – we can relax in how things are, and laugh even and find it funny. We don't have to be too serious about it.

The way we meditate is important but the focus of meditation is not that important. There are many different ways. Some focus on breathing or on something pure like a deity. You can focus on a Bodhisattva or a Buddha; it is nice to focus on something positive and good. You can use the Virgin Mary or Jesus Christ also. I think that is completely okay. The focus of the meditation is just a method to bring your mind back from distraction.

We are so used to distraction. The mind is so busy, so untamed. In a few seconds it is somewhere else. And then we are not relaxing, we are not being natural, we are reacting in our usual mind-poison way. Meditation is trying to change that habit a little bit and learn how to let be, how to be natural in a conscious way, in a deliberate way.

If we are completely distracted, it is not meditation. Just like if we are asleep, it is not meditation. So therefore we need to bring the mind back. We don't have to again pull and push. We just have to remember whatever we are being conscious about: an object, an imagined or visualised image or our breathing, or anything. It doesn't matter what the thing is. When you remember it and come back, then you are back and conscious. You don't need to do anything else. You can just be conscious of *nowness*.

Questions: Meditation

Student: Should one meditate every day or every week?

Rinpoche: I think the more you can meditate, the better it is. But not like '*I have* to meditate four hours every day,' or 'Today I did half an hour less. It's very bad.' Then it doesn't work very well. As long as you can do it in a relaxed way, in a joyful way, in a way which is not too much of a burden, then the more you do it, the better it is. There is nothing wrong with it, it doesn't have any negative effect, *unless you take it too seriously*. If you take it too strongly and too seriously then it can make you more stressed. And if it makes you more stressed, it doesn't work; it's no longer meditation.

Student: How can I meditate when I am disturbed by intense pain or when I cannot sit because of an illness? Can I use the pain for the practice?

Rinpoche: Yes, actually you can. You can let your mind settle on the pain and that sensation - the actual sensation of pain - the reality. You focus very minutely where the sensation is. If there is a pain here, then you focus not just in the general area, but more and more precisely focus on where the pain is. Your focus is very relaxed and not tight in any way. Your mind can still be spacious even though you are focusing on a particular place. Wherever there is sensation, you just focus directly on that very sensation.

After a while you might find the pain or the sensation is not there anymore; you might find it is now here... or here... or wherever. You follow it. You let your mind only focus on the sensation of the pain. When you focus where you feel the pain is but then you find it is no longer there, again you might find it somewhere else. You go through this process again and again. And when you get tired with it, you let your mind completely relax and rest.

Student: When I am meditating, a lot of images appear. Should I take these as hints for me as to what I should do in my daily life, as advice or something like that?

Rinpoche: You should not do anything. Just keep on meditating. When you meditate it is relaxed, lots of different things can come up. Sometimes very good experiences can come up, sometimes not so nice experiences can come up. Sometimes good images can come up, and not good images can come up. Whatever comes, it is just an arising, it is just a manifestation of your mind. So, you don't have to think about it too much. You put aside all thoughts such as, 'This image is coming up, so maybe I have to do this.' You just go on meditating, letting all these things come and go, not thinking too much about whether this is good or bad.

Working Skilfully

Understanding samsara

We have been talking about how to transform the negative emotions into wisdom. We have tried to see what we mean by these terms. We have also tried to see how, when we have the insight of wisdom or the experience of wisdom, then disturbed emotions cease to exist, they disappear for a while. If we experience wisdom fully, then the negative emotions would not be there. But this does not mean that the moment you have a little understanding or a little experience, then all negative things and the samsaric state of mind completely disappear.

In fact, it is extremely important to understand samsara. What does samsara mean? In Buddhism, we have many teachings on renouncing samsara and these are of great importance, but we need to be clear that renouncing samsara does not mean leaving everything behind, sitting somewhere and doing nothing. Renouncing samsara does not necessarily mean to own nothing and go and live in a cave. That may be renunciation of samsara also, but it may also not be renunciation of samsara.

When renunciation of samsara is discussed, there are two parts. The first is the understanding that samsara is a state of mind and not a location. If we are deluded and have the obscurations we were talking about earlier - the kleshas and habitual tendencies - then our mind is confused and we experience disturbed emotions. The samsaric state of mind is the state of mind in which there is confusion and misunderstanding, thus creating the negative emotions and consequently, suffering. That is the samsaric state of mind.

Enlightenment or nirvana is the opposite of samsara. Our mind is clear after we have completely done away with the obscurations, after we have uprooted the misunderstandings, the wrong way of seeing things, and consequently, the negative emotions and other hindrances have been eliminated. Then we are free from fear, free from suffering. That is enlightenment.

Samara is a state of mind of suffering and pain, a state of mind that is deluded, unclear, confused and ignorant. This is the ground upon which all negative emotions are produced and cultivated. Renunciation means wanting to get out of that state of mind, wanting to eradicate these problems, wanting to get rid of delusions and misery. That is the first thing - the thought that I want to get out of this samsaric state of mind because here there are lots of problems.

The second point is that there must be the understanding and conviction that there is a possibility to get rid of all this, to get out of this state of mind. That is renunciation. Renunciation has nothing to do with renouncing the world. The more one works on renunciation, the more compassion one has for other beings. Therefore, we are not leaving anybody behind nor turning our backs on the world.

Renunciation does not mean I do not care for anybody, that I just care for myself, that I am going into a cave and will drop all my relationships and responsibilities. Rather, we have the determination to say, 'I do not want to be entrapped in this state of mind, which again and again produces suffering because it is controlled by negative emotions. I know there is a way to get out of this frame of mind and this is what I choose to do.' That is renunciation.

From the Buddhist point of view, it is very important to really want to have this benevolent mind or *aspiration*. Then the state of renunciation becomes the starting-point. You see the priorities and know what needs to be done. So, now, trying to work on our negative emotions by having a sense of renunciation becomes our most important aim. From all Buddhist views, not only from the Mahayana and Vajrayana point of view, the foremost thing we try to work on is our negative emotions. And this is a very difficult enterprise because they are at our very core.

Any practice we do in Buddhism - whether it is meditation or any other practice - should be directed towards this goal. Otherwise there is no point to the practice. Even the prostrations we do are directed towards eliminating the negative emotions. They are especially targeted to be helpful against pride. We do prostrations to show respect and veneration, submission and openness. We bow down to somebody and that is completely the opposite of arrogance. For some people it is difficult to bow down to others. We need to know this focus and keep it in mind. We target our pride and arrogance and generate humility and respect in our mind. If that was not happening then the prostrations would be useless.

Letting go

Making offerings in the rituals is also a means of diminishing and eliminating negative emotions. Making offerings is giving, learning to let go. In Buddhist practice there is letting go of positive things and there is letting go of negative things. Making offerings is practising letting go of positive things. And there are many practices which help us learn to let go of negative things, like the purification practice of Vajrasattva. We often think that we are attached to good things and want to give up negative things, but this is not always the case. We are attached to so many things, because of our habits - both nice things and not so nice things.

There was once a Tibetan living in the place I came from. He lived along the river in the worst imaginable place. It is situated in a narrow valley between two mountains and there is no view of anything but the dark cliffs on both sides. The sun never shines there, so it is a very dreary place. This fellow went on pilgrimage to Lhasa and all over Tibet. When he returned he said, 'I travelled all over the world, and there is no place better than this sweet home!' He was simply accustomed to it.

There is another story that tells how somebody went to hell and was there for a long, long time - he had been really bad! After many, many Kalpas, he had served his time and was leaving the hell realm. He was going up to the white light or something like that, and he looked down and said to those left behind, 'Please, save my seat, don't let anybody else sit in my place!'

These stories demonstrate getting attached to things that are negative. We often get attached to feelings of hurt, to painful feelings and to things that are not nice or good. We get stuck and hold on to such an object firmly. We refuse to let it go and there is no way of getting out of the situation because we cling on to it. The more we focus on that object, the stronger our clinging becomes. If we focus our attention on something intensely, then it becomes enormous. If I have a problem and think of nothing else but that problem, then it becomes huge, even though it may be minute. In this way, we often get things out of proportion.

The princess and her tail

There is a story about a princess who had something in her eye. She was very worried and always rubbing it, so it never healed. She was very concerned. No doctor could help her. After a long time, the king proclaimed, 'Whoever can heal the princess will receive a great reward.' Then, somebody came who wasn't a doctor, but a very clever person.

He saw the princess and looked very sad and concerned. He told her, 'The eye isn't the problem, it is nothing. But there is a big problem coming.'

When she asked, 'What is the problem?' he answered, 'Oh, it is so serious. I don't think I should tell you, otherwise I will be punished.'

The king, queen and princess all pleaded, saying, 'Oh no, you won't be punished. We guarantee that nothing will happen to you. Just tell us the problem.' So, the man said, 'The eye is not the problem, the eye will heal very quickly, but you are going to grow a tail. The princess is going to grow a tail! It will be so, so long. It will be nine fathoms long. That is the problem.'

'If you notice it when it first comes out, then there may be a treatment,' he said.

Now the princess was very concerned, always touching her back, and very soon she forgot about her eye. In a few days, her eye had healed completely. But she did not grow a tail.

When she asked the man, 'Why isn't a tail growing?'

He enquired instead, 'Oh, your eye is all right?'

'Yes, my eye is all right. But what about the tail?'

'Actually I had to divert your attention and stop you touching your eyes all the time, in order to allow your eye to heal,' he responded. 'No tail is going to grow.'

If we are concerned about something and continuously and obsessively focus our attention upon it then it becomes an overwhelming problem. We must learn to recognise this and to let go.

Seeing our true nature

Two things that are very important from the Buddhist point of view are *accumulating the positive* and *letting go of the negative*. These are known as accumulation and purification. We have to check if any practice we do is effective in diminishing negative habits and increasing positive ones. If the practice we do is not working here, then it is not useful; but if it helps this, it is real practice.

We were looking at meditation earlier. This was *shiné* or *shamatha* meditation, sometimes translated as calm-abiding meditation. Every meditation is steered towards this in some way, especially at the start. It is practised in order to calm and clear the mind, to allow the mind to be at peace. As the mind becomes more relaxed, it becomes clearer and calmer, and disturbed emotions decrease. This is a very good basis for the second kind of meditation, which is insight meditation.

Calm-abiding meditation is very important and can produce very positive results, but it is never regarded as bringing us fully to the enlightened state of being. Calm-abiding meditation is used as a means. It is not the end goal and doesn't completely transform you. It is insight meditation which has the potential to bring complete transformation, because it is through this practice that you gain insight.

You come to see your true nature, seeing yourself truly and directly. That is the way one transforms the samsaric state of mind into the enlightened state of mind. This is a most important distinction. Real transformation will only occur where there is profound understanding through the practice of insight meditation.

What then can we do at this moment, when a disturbed emotion strongly arises? We don't try to push it away, feeling like we shouldn't let this happen. But we also don't follow after it, or let it take over by getting angry or whatever. What we can do at the moment is to become aware of the emotion coming up and just relax into that state of mind. We need to have the discipline and awareness to completely let it be.

What happens when we can achieve that? All the emotions are built upon tension, upon focusing on the object of the emotion, as well as other factors. If we just relax, then the ground upon which the emotion grows is pulled away. The emotion can no longer be maintained in that moment and, therefore, just fizzles out. Then the energy remains, but without any negativity.

That experience is sometimes called the transformation of the negative into wisdom. If anger arises but doesn't overcome us, it is experienced as what is often defined as mirror-like wisdom. All emotions become different types of wisdom when transformed. It is essentially the same process. If we release the emotion, natural wisdom can manifest instead. A different aspect of wisdom is there for each emotion we truly let go of with awareness.

The five mind wisdoms

Emotions arise as our reaction to perceptions and forms. It is only because our mind is unable to see perfectly clearly, like a mirror, that we experience anger. When the mind is unable to see clearly, then we feel frustrated because its natural state is to be clear. The anger *is* the frustration we have at not being able to experience the wisdom mind.

The five mind poisons are all frustrations at not being able to achieve the five mind wisdoms. If we are able to *fully* experience any of the mind poisons, however, it is no longer a poison - it evaporates. In the same way as anger becomes mirror-like wisdom:

- Anger and aversion become Mirror-like Wisdom
- Desire and attachment become Discriminating Awareness Wisdom
- Ignorance becomes All-encompassing Wisdom
- Jealousy becomes All-accomplishing Wisdom
- Pride becomes the Wisdom of Equanimity

The way you allow this to happen is to become aware of the emotion coming up and relax directly into that state of mind. This is very effective and very strong and I think the highest or most accomplished way of dealing with the emotions. But first we need to have some understanding of practising relaxation, some understanding of these types of meditation, which are a means of looking at ourselves.

Then we also need discipline. In all Vajrayana practices, subtle discipline is the most important factor. We can take any moment and any action as a practice, but we need discipline. If we don't have discipline, then we are not practising. We need subtle discipline and awareness in order to take anything that comes as a practice.

Those are the main points. If you are able to achieve this and have confidence that you can deal with any emotion that arises, whether anger, fear or whatever, then you are sure that there is no need to be overpowered by an emotion. You are able to control it. You know that you can relax into any emotion. The moment you are sure that you can control any emotion, then you lose the fear and can almost play with whatever emotion arises. Then you become a real Vajrayana practitioner, which requires both understanding and discipline.

It is true that emotions can be very strong, so strong that they manifest on the physical level. Your eyes may be almost popping out of your head with anger or you may be as white as a sheet with fear. But it doesn't mean you are unable to do anything about even these emotions. It is constantly repeated that we need to work slowly and step-by-step.

It is difficult when an emotion is very strong but this is what practice is for. It doesn't mean that negative emotions will never arise again, and it also doesn't mean that when they come, you need to frown upon yourself or feel bad. If we have a negative emotion we don't have to panic or feel that we can't do anything about it. We just work on them slowly.

Whether it is a disturbed emotion arising either in you or in others, try not to hold onto it, just let it be. Every emotion is like that: it comes and goes and comes and goes. So, the technique or wisdom of the practice is that you let it come and you let it go.

However, we need to be clear that letting go does not mean pushing something away. If you try to push an emotion away, it becomes stronger and sticks to you. The more forcefully you push something, the harder it becomes. Sometimes it is difficult to let go and people try to push. Pushing and letting go are not identical.

The story of the tar baby is just like this. If you slap the tar baby, your hand gets stuck in it. If you pretend that it is not there and you want to pass by, you step on it and get stuck in it. Whatever you do, you somehow get stuck in the tar baby. It is like that with emotions. If you push the emotions away, you get stuck in them. Of course, if you hold on to them you get stuck too!

'Letting go' is an expression used quite often in Buddhism. It is very important to let go. But you have to know exactly what letting go means. Sometimes I feel that letting go is understood as meaning pushing very hard. It is often misinterpreted this way. It is not about letting go while thinking, 'Go!' It may be better to say *letting be*. It is just about *being*. If something comes, it's all right. When it goes, that's all right too. You are not reacting too much, but letting be, letting go.

Transforming Emotions

We have covered how we start to address emotions by developing our understanding and a clear, positive attitude. Then we looked at how we can bring some stability and flexibility to our mind through meditation, which can progress to bring deeper and deeper insight into the nature of emotions and ourselves. Through this we have seen how we can work with emotions as they arise and try to release them. There are three different approaches we can use to transform emotions in this way:

Generating the opposite feeling

This is the first or easiest method. Looking at hatred, for example. When working on the emotion of hatred or anger, one tries to generate compassion. When we have the experience of love and compassion, in that moment we cannot have hatred and anger. So, the practice of generating the opposite is a method to deal with negative emotions.

We think, 'Why am I angry?' and we find we are angry because somebody did or said something against us. Alright; but why did he or she do this to me? Because he or she was angry. But why was he or she angry? Because he or she was in trouble, had had a fight with his wife or her husband or something bad had happened.

Now we can understand that this person was unhappy at that time. They were suffering and had problems. You know from your own experience that if everything is nice, there is no reason to be angry. You don't get angry for fun. You don't say, 'I had such a nice time when I was angry!' Therefore, if someone is angry, that person is suffering. When we understand that someone is suffering and having problems we don't usually get angry, rather we sympathise or empathise.

This is compassion in a way, the wish that there be no suffering. This is the first method of transforming our negative emotions into positive feelings, trying to generate the opposite. By generating the positive aspect, the negative is solved and temporarily resolved.

Seeing the illusory nature of things

The second method is seeing the illusory nature of all things. We look at the anger or whatever negative emotion arises. We also look at the person who is having the emotion and we ask why is this emotion arising? Towards whom or what is this emotion directed? We see all these are illusory and transitory events. None of them lasts all the time. We thereby understand how everything is interdependent.

None of these emotions stands on their own. There is nothing very solid there, it is coming and going. But if we hold on to it again and again, it can seem or feel as if it is very solid. We need to see that these emotions are not solid and rigid but are something flowing, something coming again and again but not being there all the time.

In Buddhist terms this is what is known as seeing *emptiness* – seeing that everything is interdependent and nothing exists independently on its own. Understanding interdependence is not an easy practice but if you can reach that kind of understanding, this is another way to transform the emotions.

You look at yourself, at your thoughts and emotions and reactions, and whether there is anything besides that, or behind that. This is what you are. You are your body, your mind, your thoughts, your emotions. When you learn how to let things be, and can be totally relaxed in the present moment, you learn slowly how to deal with your emotions. In this way you learn about yourself, what you really are. You come to know the nature of your thoughts and emotions and reactions, you come to know yourself.

'What you are' is not something concrete like 'I am like this' and nothing else. You are like everything else: something that is a little conscious with lots of thoughts, lots of emotions, lots of doubts, lots of fear; all this is you and it is like all of us. It is not a realisation like 'I have found myself, yes, I am this.' It is nothing like that. But it is okay. Whatever you are, that is what you are. You don't need to try to find exactly what that is. Whatever you are, you relax in that. You accept whatever is there.

Directly relaxing into emotions

The last method is directly relaxing into the emotions in just the same way as we have already been discussing. It is directly transforming the negative emotions into wisdom. It includes not just negative emotions but every emotion. Whatever emotion, whatever thought arises in the mind, just relax into that and let it be.

The whole point is you are in charge and you can experience going beyond and above the emotions a little bit. If you have the right discipline, instead of following an emotion when it comes up, you can just look back at your own mind. You look back at the mind that is angry or the mind that is proud or desiring. If you can do that, in that moment you break the sequence, you break the thread. You look back, and within that you relax.

It is said the emotion is then *liberated by itself as it arises* which means that then there is nothing there. You look back and the anger, or whatever emotion was arising, kind of dissipates, because there is no thing called 'anger.' The anger has to be fed by the continuum of the thoughts of anger, whatever thoughts were giving rise to the anger.

Therefore when you look back at your own mind you break that continuum and you are left with a kind of clarity or a clear void. There is a clarity but there is no longer any force. It is like when you take the wood away from a fire, it dies down. In the same way, there is no force to burn and the emotion dissipates.

If you become more accustomed and stable in the practice, then it is said that the emotions and negative feelings that arise become like a thief entering an empty house. If you have an empty house, the thief can come and go without you needing to worry, because there is nothing to steal. Likewise, whatever emotion comes or goes, it doesn't matter, because you are not bothered by it.

Through these methods you can come to experience that emotions and all these things do not really control you. You do not need to be controlled by anything. You are free, because you don't have to react. You do not have to fear. You do not have to hold on to anything.

The most important thing to learn is that you do not have to react with aversion or attachment. That is realisation. When you learn that a little bit, in a practical way, you know you are free. You are not the slave of your emotions, you are not the slave of anything.

The more strongly and experientially we learn that, the more liberated we become. Liberation and realisation are always connected. The more we realise, the more liberated we become. Because the more we see what we really are - what our thoughts, emotions and reactions are - the more we are freed from their clutches.

We do not need to run after anything or run away from anything. We do not need to be afraid of things or our own emotions; we do not need to react to them. Liberation and realisation are what we call enlightenment. Sometimes we call it enlightenment because it's a complete clarity. You see very clearly, not in an intellectual way but in an experiential way.

Clarifying Practice

Question: Working in this moment

Student: Normally, when negative emotions arise, you are carried away in that moment. How can one develop the ability not to suppress nor be carried away by an emotion the moment it arises?

Rinpoche: That is why I spoke about discipline and awareness, which have to be developed. The best thing in the end is to practice what we have discussed as transforming negative emotions into wisdom. That is ultimately the best way, but it is not the easiest way in the beginning. Therefore, we have to first learn and train. We have to train in many different ways.

The first point is to recognise a negative emotion as a negative emotion, understanding that it is something that will lead us to problems and suffering. A disturbed emotion will never lead us to anything good, rather to something not so nice. When we understand that deeply, then we can continue our training.

We can start by using our awareness and being mindful. This is a very simple but most effective and fundamental practice. The story of the shepherd shows how this is so.

The shepherd

Once there was a shepherd who was tending his herd in the mountains. A renowned lama lived in a cave nearby. The shepherd had heard many things about him, that he was a highly realised lama. Students came from faraway places to see him. One day the shepherd visited the lama and said, 'I am a simple shepherd. I know nothing, I am illiterate, but I want to do some Dharma practice. Would you give me a practice that requires no understanding, knowledge or education, just a simple practice a most ignorant person could do?'

The lama responded, 'Take two small bags and fill one with white pebbles and the other with black pebbles. When you sit on a rock while watching over the sheep, keep the two bags near you and just look at yourself, watch your mind. If a negative emotion arises in your mind, take a black pebble and place it on your left side. If a good emotion arises in your mind, then place a white pebble at your right side. Just do that and nothing else.'

The shepherd did as the lama suggested. He filled his two bags with black and white pebbles and watched his mind. During his practice he noted - one black pebble, two black pebbles, ten black pebbles, fifty black pebbles. No white pebbles! At the end, there were only one or two white pebbles. So, he was very worried and concluded, 'This is not good. This is a very bad practice.'

He returned to the lama and complained, 'This is not good. The black pebbles are growing into a mountain and there are only two or three white pebbles.'

The lama answered, 'It doesn't matter. Just keep on doing that. Place the pebbles in the bags and start anew every day.'

The shepherd did as he was told, again and again. Slowly, slowly, after several months, the white pile grew and the black pile became smaller.

That is how the practice works and that is the message of this story. In daily life, we don't have a specific time when we practice. Whatever we do, whether we are washing the dishes, cooking dinner, driving our car or looking after children, from time to time, whenever we are aware we look at our mind.

We can't do this all the time, but whenever we have the chance or opportunity, we look to see what state of mind we are in. Then we become aware. If something nice is going on, then there is no tension and we are more peaceful. We have a good feeling and notice that it is nice, like placing a white pebble. If our state of mind is not like that and we feel tense and negative, then we can try to apply whatever technique we know, for example to come to see the good sides of whatever is happening and how circumstances inter-relate.

If you are aware you feel angry or hurt or rejected or unhappy, then you are also aware that those feelings may depend upon certain specific circumstances. And they may be circumstances which you cannot change, because usually we cannot change circumstances.

We continue contemplating and see that our way of dealing with circumstances is actually down to our own way of reacting. If we react negatively, then who is the one who suffers? I am the one who suffers. Maybe others do too, but I am the first who suffers and who will suffer the most. Therefore, I should be determined not to react like that, because it is foolish. I would only be punishing myself. It is not the solution and nothing good will arise from such a reaction. I will not allow myself to feel badly, understanding that there is nothing to feel bad about. Things are like that and it is all right. If I don't make myself happy, then who will?

Somebody gave me a postcard once which read, *There is no way to happiness, happiness is the way*. The Buddha was supposed to have said this. Happiness is the way. Joy is something that you just develop. This is something we always speak about in Buddhism.

When you have a negative emotion the only solution is to catch hold of it and see its destructive side. Then it will change. Maybe it will not disappear then and there, but this is a way of working on it, slowly. We first try to develop a little awareness. Then, when our awareness and mindfulness become stronger, we can catch a negative emotion even if it is strong. We can experiment with this practice.

Sometimes negative emotions are purposefully generated during practice. This gives us a chance to look at the anger or whatever emotion has been encouraged to arise. For example, Chögyam Trungpa Rinpoche developed a practice based around the Six Realms. Each realm is associated with a different emotion. The human realm is associated with desire; the animal realm is associated with ignorance; and so on. Chögyam Trungpa Rinpoche designed small rooms, each in a different colour, which would encourage different emotions to arise. Each room provided a different atmosphere.

The practice is to spend some time in each room in a specific posture, which is also chosen to encourage that particular emotion to come up. Then one can look at the emotion, experience it fully and practice dealing with it[2]. What all such exercises are designed to do is to allow us to look at emotions and learn to let them be.

Question: Seeing through illusion

Student: Sometimes we feel happy about something or somebody because we see only what we want to see. Then later we discover that things aren't the way we had supposed and hoped them to be. Searching for happiness itself seems to be an illusion and not a reality.

Rinpoche: What do you mean by happiness?
Student: Non-suffering.

Rinpoche: So, non-suffering is an illusion? What about suffering?
Student: Everything is an illusion.

Rinpoche: If you really and very deeply find that everything is an illusion, then you have found happiness. Because if you deeply and experientially find that suffering is an illusion, then you also find that happiness is an illusion. You discover that there is no need to struggle for happiness, nor to struggle to escape from unhappiness.

If you feel this experientially, then that is called 'happiness', because there is no struggle in this state. There is complete peace and no fear.

That is what happiness is. But it is difficult to first realise that it is an illusion. This is one of the main practices when working with emotions, to find the illusory nature of all things. But it is difficult to do.

Practise what you understand

We work on our emotions slowly and gradually, step-by-step. We can use any or all of the methods given as we choose: we can use generating the opposite feeling; seeing the illusory nature of things and directly relaxing into emotions. The important thing is to start with whatever I can understand, whatever is easy for me to do.

Sometimes people ask me what is the best way for them. I always say it is not necessarily the most difficult or the most profound way that is the best, because you have to understand it first. Whatever I understand most and whatever I can connect with is the first thing I have to work with. If I understand it then I will do it, because I know how to do it. If I don't understand the method I can't do it even if I want to, so it doesn't work for me. Therefore, I try to work on the simplest things.

When we listen to teachings or practices, if it is something that is easy to understand, we might tend to put it on one side: 'Okay, I understand that.' Then when we hear something that we don't understand, something very difficult and complicated, we think, 'Oh, I really don't understand that,' and we keep it over on another side. Then, at the end of many years of receiving teachings and reading books and all these things, we find we have done nothing with the teachings we actually understood. We have just kept them over to one side. All the easy things we have kept over to this side. And all the difficult things we did not understand we have put over on the other side.

I find I never used the things I could have used to work on myself and transform myself. In the end nothing has worked on me and I have not changed at all. None of it affected me in any way!

So it is important to *practise* what we understand, to remind ourselves again and again and to integrate the teachings with our life, day by day. Slowly it seeps in and becomes more than just an intellectual understanding. It goes from our head to our heart, which is usually said to be the longest journey ever. That journey has to be made by repeatedly doing, again and again.

Sometimes when a strong emotion arises, it is helpful just to let it be and not to react for some time. Take a deep breath in and out slowly. Do this three times. Everything comes and goes and that is something we need to really understand, that nothing remains. When we can let an emotion go, when we can let it be, then it is all right. Anything negative or positive that comes, goes again. When we understand that nothing lasts, then we can be more relaxed.

Question: Eliminating anger and fear

Student: I would like to get rid of my anger and fear but isn't that, in itself, aversion? I am wondering, does an enlightened being still experience negative emotions?

Rinpoche: In answer to the second part of the question, it depends on how enlightened they are!

It is true we want to get rid of anger and fear and negative feelings. We don't want to have them. That is why we try to work on them. Then we realise, in the course of practising, that we cannot work on these emotions by just not wanting them. Not wanting to have fear will not get rid of fear. We have to learn a way of skilfully dissolving the fear or skilfully transforming it. We have been talking about the different ways to do this.

First there is the importance of seeing the uselessness of feeling these emotions: this is attitude. But this does not totally uproot the emotions. So we need to learn how to relax. When I have fear and it is arising and I think, 'Ah, quick, I must think about.... my breathing.' And then I am breathing very deliberately and concentrating on that. It works to some extent because then my mind is diverted to something else and I am not concentrating on the fear. I let the fear go in that very moment. This is using the principle of calm-abiding meditation. It works in the short term, but it does not uproot the fear.

If we can just look at the fear and *in that very fear*, we can relax; this is more difficult to do but it is how to take out the root of the fear. We are not running away. We are not trying to push it away. We are just deeply, deeply relaxing in what is arising, so the fear cannot hold on anymore. We have freed ourselves from the grasping of fear. If we really learn how to do that, then the fear loses its grasp on us. It loses its grip on us. And we have learnt how to deal with fear.

When we have learnt that way deeply, then we can 'self-liberate' fear. Then it is no big deal. Whatever is arising, whether it is fear or anger or whatever, we can self-liberate it. We can self-liberate any thoughts or emotions. That is extremely important.

Student: Can you describe the technique to do this a bit more? Because the problem I find is that when I look at the fear I get wrapped up in it and my mind continues the fear?

Rinpoche: When we have fear, for instance, we are concentrating on what we have fear of. So we are concentrating 'out' – this enemy, this ghost, this problem etc. When I say 'relax in it,' I am not advising to relax on that. I look at my fear itself, at my experience of fear itself - the feeling of fear, the back of my neck tingling or whatever. I look back at that and in that feeling of fear, I relax. When I do that I am not looking outwardly at what I fear. I am just looking at the experience of fear and relaxing in that.

Student: So the focus is more on the sensation?

Rinpoche: Yes, it is focusing on the sensation of fear, not on the object of fear.

Final Words

Happiness is the way

I was saying earlier, there is no road leading to happiness, *happiness is the way*. I think this is very important. Usually when we do something, we do it expecting something in return. That is our usual attitude. It is important for us to get something back. But sometimes it does not work like that.

Most of the time, your present state of mind is the cause for your next state of mind. You think you want to get happiness so therefore you will do this particular thing. A few days later, you may have accomplished this goal, but become tense again anyway, because you have become used to that attitude. We are so used to leading our lives with the expectation that first I will do this and then I will get that. Actually, if we want to be more joyful, we have to *be* more joyful!

This is one of the main practices, especially in the Vajrayana, that you just have to be. It is also very important to understand that we become what we have become used to doing. If we are always frowning, our face becomes like that; and if we are always smiling, then our face becomes like that. That is the reason why, if we want to be happier and more relaxed, then we try to be like that now and not wait until something happens - like until lots of rainbows and flowers shower upon us!

It is very important to understand that we and everybody else have problems all the time. Who doesn't have problems? It is very unlikely that you can find anybody who has no problems. But then when we have a problem we focus our attention on that problem so intensely, we make it bigger in the process, and become totally absorbed in it. We focus all our attention on the problem and we can't see anything else. It becomes our whole reality. If there is nothing else but the problem for us, then everything is a problem and nothing is nice.

Therefore, we have to expand our view more and more. We have problems and they will never totally vanish because other problems will always pop up again and again. For instance, maybe I have problems but right now, sitting here, I feel good. The better I feel, the more joyful I am because I am not concentrating on the problems I have. Of course, you have to take problems into consideration in order to solve them; it is not possible to ignore them. But at times when it is not necessary to consider and become involved with a problem, then just relax and let things be.

The more relaxed you are, the less tense you are and the more joyful you become. And the more joyful you feel, the more joyful you become! It becomes a habit, a pattern. It is the same with hatred. Everything grows and increases the more and more one becomes accustomed to it. So really we just need to be and let things be.

The rich men and the fisherman

Once, two rich men were rushing to go sailing on their beautiful yacht. A fisherman was sitting on the beach with his fishing-rod. The two men stopped in their tracks and approached him. They asked him, 'What are you doing? Why aren't you doing something useful?'

The fisherman responded, 'What do you think I should do?'

They shouted, 'You should work. You are in the way!'

'Well,' asked the fisherman, 'what will happen if I work?'

'You will get money,' insisted the two.

The fisherman inquired, 'What should I do when I have money?'

The rich men told him, 'Then you can do more work so that you can get more money.'

And the fisherman asked again, 'What should I do when I get more money?'

'Then you will become rich and can invest your money,' agreed the two.

'What should I do when I become rich?' asked the fisherman.

The two men beamed, 'Then you can do whatever you like.'

The fisherman nodded, saying, 'Ah, yes, and that is what I am doing right now!'

Conclusion

The practice of Buddhism is about learning to deal with negative or disturbed emotions. We can't accomplish this all at once. Firstly, we need to understand the importance of working with the emotions, and then we slowly work on them. In Buddhism we always talk about compassion, and this is the most important thing to develop. But we also always want to do things quickly, and this is not always possible. If we try to be very compassionate all at once, for example, we may head towards problems only to discover we are not capable of solving them at all. Therefore, we first need to learn to be compassionate with ourselves and work on that.

It is also important to understand that practice doesn't only consist of formal meditation but embraces all aspects of life. While it is not possible to eradicate all negative things, we can still try to create a pleasant environment with fewer problems, and we can try to appreciate a simple life without too many complications. Through this we create more harmony.

Harmony is very important. With a little bit of harmony within, and a little bit of harmony around yourself, then you already have a better life. If the five elements within your body are in harmony, then you enjoy good health. If there is harmony in the community, then you have peace. And if there is harmony in your mind, then you have happiness. I think aiming for a little more harmony is a good place to start.

What is happiness?

To be happy is to be free from fear
To be happy is to self liberate your thoughts and emotions
To be happy is to learn how to enjoy the presence
To be happy is to know that anything is great
To be happy is to be in nowness with full clarity
To be happy is to not look forward for a happiness
This is happiness
Now is happiness
Anytime is happiness
There is nothing but happiness
It is nothing special to be happy
What a freedom not to have to run after happiness

Ringu Tulku

Dedication

All my babbling,
In the name of Dharma
Has been set down faithfully
By my dear students of pure vision.

I pray that at least a fraction of the wisdom
Of those enlightened teachers
Who tirelessly trained me
Shines through this mass of incoherence.

May the sincere efforts of all those
Who have worked tirelessly
Result in spreading the true meaning of Dharma
To all who are inspired to know.

May this help dispel the darkness of ignorance
In the minds of all living beings
And lead them to complete realisation
Free from all fear.

Ringu Tulku

Glossary & Notes

Bodhisattva (Sanskrit; *changchub sempa* Tibetan) comes from the root *Bodh* which means to know, to have the full understanding. The term describes a being who has made a commitment to work for the benefit of other beings to bring them to a state of lasting peace and happiness and freedom from all suffering. A Bodhisattva themselves does not have to be a Buddhist but can come from any spiritual tradition or none. The key thing is that they have this compassionate wish to free beings from suffering, informed by the wisdom of knowing this freedom is possible.

Chögyam Trungpa Rinpoche [1939 – 1987] was a Buddhist teacher of the Kagyu lineage. He was instrumental in bringing the Tibetan teachings into the West, particularly America, where he founded the Naropa Institute, Shambhala Training and the Nalanda Translation Committee. He also headed numerous meditation centres in America and Europe and is the author of many books on Buddhist philosophy and practice. He was not only a meditation master and scholar but also a poet and artist.

Deity in Buddhism refers to seeing the pure state of reality. Different 'deities' may be represented in different forms to bring out certain aspects but what they are all getting at is seeing the pure state; by which we mean the state that does not bind us or make any problems for us and which therefore liberates us.

Dharma (Sanskrit; *chö* Tibetan) The word *dharma* has many uses. In its widest sense it means all that can be known. Its other main meaning (and the meaning indicated by the word in this text) is the teachings of the Buddha; also called the Buddhadharma. This refers to the entire body of Buddhist teachings and includes literal teachings and that which is learnt through practising the teachings.

Emptiness (*shunyata* Sanskrit; *tong pa nyi* Tibetan) The Buddha taught in the second turning of the wheel of Dharma, that all phenomena have no real, independent existence of their own. They only appear to exist as separate, nameable entities because of how we commonly, conceptually, see things. But, in themselves, all things are 'empty' of inherent existence. This includes our 'self', which we habitually unconsciously mistake to be an independently-existing, separate phenomenon. Instead, everything exists in an interdependent way and this is what the term *emptiness* refers to. 'Emptiness does not mean there is nothing; emptiness means the way everything is, the way everything magically manifests'.[3]

Fathom is a measurement of length, originally based on the distance between the fingertips with the arms outstretched, a little under two meters. The term derives from an old English word meaning embracing arms or a pair of outstretched arms.

Five elements, according to the Tibetan system, are made up of the four elements of Earth, Water, Fire and Wind, together in Space, the fifth element. All manifest life is comprised of these five elements and their interaction. The aspect of any form that is solid is its Earth element. The Water element is its fluidity and cohesion. Fire includes the qualities of warmth and ripening. Wind is the aspect of movement. The dimension in which these four can manifest and come together to create life, is the element of Space. Harmony of these five elements together brings health and disharmony brings illness. Dissolution of the elements brings death.

Guru Padmasambhava (**Guru Rinpoche**) is the name of the great 8th century Indian mahasiddha teacher known as the 'Lotus Born.' He came to Tibet from India in order to tame negative elemental forces and spread the Buddhadharma. In particular, he taught many tantras and Vajrayana practices, and concealed many teachings to be revealed at a later time by his disciples.

Habitual tendencies (*she bye drib pa* Tibetan) Literally translated as 'obscurations of knowledge,' these refer to our propensity to act or react in certain ways, reinforced and influenced by past actions. They become ingrained in us again and again until they are habitual.

Insight meditation (*vipassana* Pali; *vipaśyanā* Sanskrit; *lhakthong* Tibetan) is usually practised after gaining some experience of 'calm-abiding' meditation (*shiné* or *shamatha*). It refers to gaining insight into your true nature, seeing yourself truly and directly, which becomes the basis for transformation.

Kagyu (Tibetan) *Ka* means oral and *gyu* means lineage; the lineage of oral transmission. Also known as the Lineage of Meaning and Blessing or the Practice Lineage. One of the four major schools of Buddhism in Tibet, it was founded in Tibet by Marpa and is headed by His Holiness Karmapa. The other three schools are the Nyingma, Sakya and Gelugpa schools.

Kalpa (Tibetan; *yuga* Sanskrit) A measure of time, an eon, which lasts in the order of millions of years, sometimes calculated to be over 4000 million years.

Karma (Sanskrit; *lay* Tibetan) literally means 'action.' It refers to the cycle of cause and effect that is set up through actions coloured or motivated by *klesha* (see below). In practice if we do something fuelled by, for example, anger or desire, it will shape our experience of the potential of our situation. It shapes the results that arise from our actions and our tendencies to do similar actions. These tendencies become totally ingrained in us and become our habitual way of being, which is our karma. While an individual's karma cannot be 'taken on' or altered by anyone else (see the story of Valmiki); it is possible for groups, families and nations to share similar or resonant karma.

Kleshas (*kleśa* Sanskrit; *nyön mong* Tibetan) refer to the mental defilements, mind poisons or negative emotions. They include any emotion or mind state that disturbs or distorts consciousness. They bring forth our experience of suffering and prevent our experience of love, joy and happiness. The three main kleshas are desire, anger and ignorance. Combinations of these give rise to the five kleshas, which are these three plus pride and envy / jealousy.

Lama (Tibetan; *guru* Sanskrit) means teacher or master. '*La*' refers to there being nobody higher in terms of spiritual accomplishment and '*ma*' refers to compassion like a mother. Thus both wisdom and compassion are brought to fruition together in the Lama.

Mahamudra (Sanskrit; *cha ja chen po* or *phyag chen* Tibetan) literally means 'Great Seal' or 'Great Symbol', referring to the way in which all phenomena are 'sealed' by the primordially perfect true nature. The term can denote the teaching, meditation practice or accomplishment of Mahamudra. The meditation consists in perceiving the mind directly rather than through what one could call the 'prism' of rational analysis, and relies on a direct introduction to the nature of the essence of the mind. The accomplishment lies in experiencing the non-duality of the phenomenal world and emptiness: perceiving how the two are not separate. This experience can also be called the union of emptiness and luminosity.

Mahayana Buddhism (*Mahayana* Sanskrit; *tek pa chen po* Tibetan) Mahayana translates as 'Great Vehicle.' This is the second vehicle of Buddhism which emphasizes the teachings on interdependence, compassion and Bodhicitta. These expand on those of the Sravakayana (the first vehicle of Buddhism which follows the basic teachings of the Buddha) through seeing the purpose of enlightenment as the liberation of all sentient beings from suffering, as well as oneself. This is the path of the Bodhisattva (see above) who vows to work towards the liberation of all sentient beings and so may also be called the Bodhisattvayana.

Maitrî (Pali; *maitreya* Sanskrit) means loving-kindness and is one of the Four Limitless Qualities, so called because we can cultivate them without limit. The other three are compassion, sympathetic joy and equanimity. Maitreya is the name of the Buddha said to be of the coming age, 'the Loving One'.

Nirvana (Sanskrit; *nyangde* Tibetan) literally means 'extinguished' and is the state of being free from all suffering. It is the opposite of samsara and arises when we have completely done away with all the obscurations, misunderstandings, negative emotions and other hindrances. When we are free from all fear and suffering and our mind is completely clear; this is enlightenment or nirvana.

Obscurations are anything that prevents us from seeing something; they block our direct and clear seeing. Whatever obscures and prevents us from seeing the true nature of something is an obscuration.

Prostrations are a physical practice whereby one places one's hands in prayer mudra (gesture) to one's head, throat and heart and then one lies prostrate and places the prayer gesture on one's head. A simpler version can include simply coming to hands and knees at this point with the head touching the floor. There are many and various interpretations of the meaning of each gesture. Essentially the first three gestures represent bringing body, speech and mind to practice. The full prostration represents completely surrendering the whole of oneself into the hands of the transformation process (or the lineage of teachers and teachings and the effect they may have on oneself). When the hands, knees and head touch the floor, this can be seen as representing the five main kleshas or negative emotions and giving them up, to allow their transformation into the five wisdoms.

Ramayana is an ancient Sanskrit epic ascribed to the sage Valmiki. It forms an important part of the Hindu canon. Valmiki is revered as the first Hindu poet who, through this epic, defined the form of Sanskrit poetry.

Renunciation is the firm wish to be free of the state of suffering that characterises the samsaric state of mind. This includes seeing that there is a possibility of achieving this and being willing to go in this way. True renunciation is renunciation of the heart and mind and does not include turning away from the world. In actuality, it increases our compassion and care for all other beings.

Samadhi (Sanskrit; *ting nge zin* Tibetan) A state of meditative absorption in which the mind rests unwaveringly.

Samsara / samsaric (Sanskrit; *kor wa* Tibetan) is the state of suffering of 'cyclic existence.' It is a state of mind of gross and / or subtle pain and dissatisfaction. It arises because the mind is deluded and unclear and thus perpetually conditioned by attachment, aggression and ignorance.

Shiné (*zhi gnas* Tibetan) or shamatha (*śamatha* Sanskrit) is calm abiding meditation; calming and stabilising the mind to bring it to a state of peace. Sometimes also called Tranquillity meditation.

Six Realms These realms of reality may describe literal places or states of mind. They are the Hell Realm, in which anger is predominant. The Hungry Ghost Realm in which greed and insatiable craving predominate. The Animal Realm in which ignorance is predominant. The God Realm in which pride is predominant. The Jealous God Realm in which jealousy is predominant. And the Human Realm in which desire is the main emotion that colours experience. This is also the only realm that brings the freedom to choose the path away from suffering.

Tantra (*gyu* Tibetan) literally means 'continuity'. In Buddhism it refers to the root texts of the Vajrayana and to the meditative practices they describe, which include mantra recitation and visualisation.

Tar baby refers to the doll made of tar and turpentine in the Uncle Remus children's stories, which was used to entrap Br'er Rabbit. The moral of the tale is that the more Br'er Rabbit fights the tar baby, the more entangled with it he becomes. In modern usage 'tar baby' refers to any 'sticky situation' that further contact can only aggravate.

Vajrasattva (Sanskrit; *dorje sempa* Tibetan) is the Buddha who particularly embodies innate purity and is associated with purification. *Vajra* means 'diamond-like' or of 'indestructible capacity' - the mythology of the vajra is that it is made of the most indestructible material, like a diamond. It can cut any other material but cannot be cut by any other material. Vajrasattva represents the enlightened state of pure being that arises when everything that confuses and obscures it, is discarded, dissolved and let go of (i.e. purified).

Vajrayana Buddhism (Sanskrit; *dorje tek pa* Tibetan) *Vajra* means 'diamond-like' or of 'indestructible capacity' and conveys a sense of what is beyond arising and ceasing and, therefore, indestructible (see *Vajrasattva* above). The Vajrayana is the third vehicle of Buddhism and incorporates and accepts all the teachings of the Sravakayana (the foundational vehicle of Buddhism which follows the basic teachings of the Buddha) and the Mahayana, or Bodhisattvayana. The Vajrayana then also includes teachings on the tantras and various skilful means. It is the method of taking the result as the path and may afford the practitioner swift progress, practised in accordance with the foundations of Buddhist approach.

Yana (Sanskrit; *tek pa* Tibetan) eg. the three yanas, the nine yanas. *Yana* means vehicle and refers to categories of Buddhist teachings that provide approaches with different emphases. The aim of such vehicles is to provide the means of 'crossing over' to the other side; transforming life from samsaric experience to an experience of enlightenment or 'clear seeing'. The different yanas provide a different view of the journey and are suitable for different practitioners.

Notes

1. Translation taken from: '*Sky Dancer: The Secret Life and Songs of the Lady Yeshe Tsogyel*' by Keith Dowman.

2. This practice has become known as 'Maitrî Space Awareness' and is taught in seminars all over the world.

3. Taken from '*Like Dreams and Clouds: Emptiness and Interdependence; Mahamudra and Dzogchen*' Heart Wisdom Series No. 4 by Ringu Tulku.

Acknowledgments

The teachings presented in this book came from various sources, before being worked gradually into the format given here. The main body of this book came from a teaching given by Ringu Tulku in 1997 at Samye Dzong in Barcelona, Spain. We express our gratitude to the members of this centre for organising this seminar and also to Gabriele Hollmann, who provided the transcript and first edit of this teaching. Further text for this book was taken from a teaching given at Dharma-Tor, Germany in 2003, and our thanks also go to those organisers and to Keith Carr, who transcribed the teaching.

Shorter extracts have been included from a number of other teachings which were consistent with the topic and added further clarification. These came from talks Ringu Tulku gave at the University of Naropa, Boulder, Colorado in 1999 (recorded by Ger Reinders); in Chichester, UK in 1999 (transcribed by Cait Collins); in London in 2006 (recorded by Bernie Hartley) and as part of the Bodhicharya online shedra teachings on the Bodhicharyavatara in 2012 (BA4Q3 transcribed by Pat Murphy).

Our thanks go to Rachel Moffitt, David Tuffield, Anna Howard and Pat Murphy, who all contributed proof reading and comments as the text progressed. Thank you to Margaret Ford, who coordinates Bodhicharya Publications and established the publishing team and Heart Wisdom Series. She also shared the poem written by Ringu Tulku included in this book. Maria Hündorf-Kaiser administrates the archives of Ringu Tulku's recorded teachings and Paul O'Connor provided the design and layout of this book. Our acknowledgments and best wishes go to everyone in this wide network and all the many students thus involved. We apologise for any errors, which are entirely our own.

Finally, our deepest gratitude goes to Ringu Tulku and the teaching lineage he brings to us. He has tirelessly shared his illumination of the teachings with so many students, in many centres over many years.

May there be great benefit.

Mary Heneghan & Marion Knight
Bodhicharya Publications
July 2012

About the Author

Ringu Tulku Rinpoche is a Tibetan Buddhist Master of the Kagyu Order. He was trained in all schools of Tibetan Buddhism under many great masters including HH the 16th Gyalwang Karmapa and HH Dilgo Khyentse Rinpoche. He took his formal education at Namgyal Institute of Tibetology, Sikkim and Sampurnananda Sanskrit University, Varanasi, India. He served as Tibetan Textbook Writer and Professor of Tibetan Studies in Sikkim for 25 years.

Since 1990, he has been travelling and teaching Buddhism and meditation in Europe, America, Canada, Australia and Asia. He participates in various interfaith and 'Science and Buddhism' dialogues and is the author of several books on Buddhist topics. These include *Path to Buddhahood, Daring Steps, The Ri-me Philosophy of Jamgon Kongtrul the Great, Confusion Arises as Wisdom*, the *Lazy Lama* series and the *Heart Wisdom* series, as well as several children's books, available in Tibetan and European languages.

He founded the organisations Bodhicharya - see www.bodhicharya.org and Rigul Trust - see www.rigultrust.org.

Other books by Ringu Tulku

PUBLISHED BY BODHICHARYA PUBLICATIONS:

The Heart Wisdom Series:

- *The Ngöndro*
  Foundation Practices of Mahamudra
- *From Milk to Yoghurt*
  A Recipe for Living and Dying
- *Like Dreams and Clouds*
  Emptiness and Interdependence;
  Mahamudra and Dzogchen
- *Dealing with Emotions*
  Scattering the Clouds
- *Journey from Head to Heart*
  Along a Buddhist Path
- *Riding Stormy Waves*
  Victory over the Maras

The Lazy Lama Series:

- *Buddhist Meditation*
- *The Four Noble Truths*
- *Refuge*
  Finding a Purpose and a Path
- *Bodhichitta*
  Awakening Compassion and Wisdom
- *Living without Fear and Anger*
- *Relaxing in Natural Awareness*

PUBLISHED BY SHAMBHALA:

- *Path to Buddhahood:* Teachings on Gampopa's 'Jewel Ornament of Liberation'
- *Daring Steps:* Traversing the Path of the Buddha
- *Mind Training*
- *The Ri-Me Philosophy of Jamgon Kongtrul the Great:*
  A Study of the Buddhist Lineages of Tibet.
- *Confusion Arises as Wisdom:* Gampopa's Heart Advice on the Path of Mahamudra.

ALSO AVAILABLE FROM RIGUL TRUST:

- *Chenrezig:* The Practice of Compassion - A Commentary
- *The Boy who had a Dream:* An illustrated book for children